CONTROL TOWERS!
WHO WORKS THERE AND WHAT THEY DO

Technology for Kids
Children's Aviation Books

All Rights reserved. No part of this book may be reproduced or used in any way or form or by any means whether electronic or mechanical, this means that you cannot record or photocopy any material ideas or tips that are provided in this book.

Copyright 2016

There are about 50000 airplanes flying across United States everyday.

But how do these airplanes keep from colliding with each other?

Have you ever wondered how an airplane knows where to land?

An Airplane has a traffic system and it is monitored by a control tower.

Every airport must have control towers. What is a Control Tower?

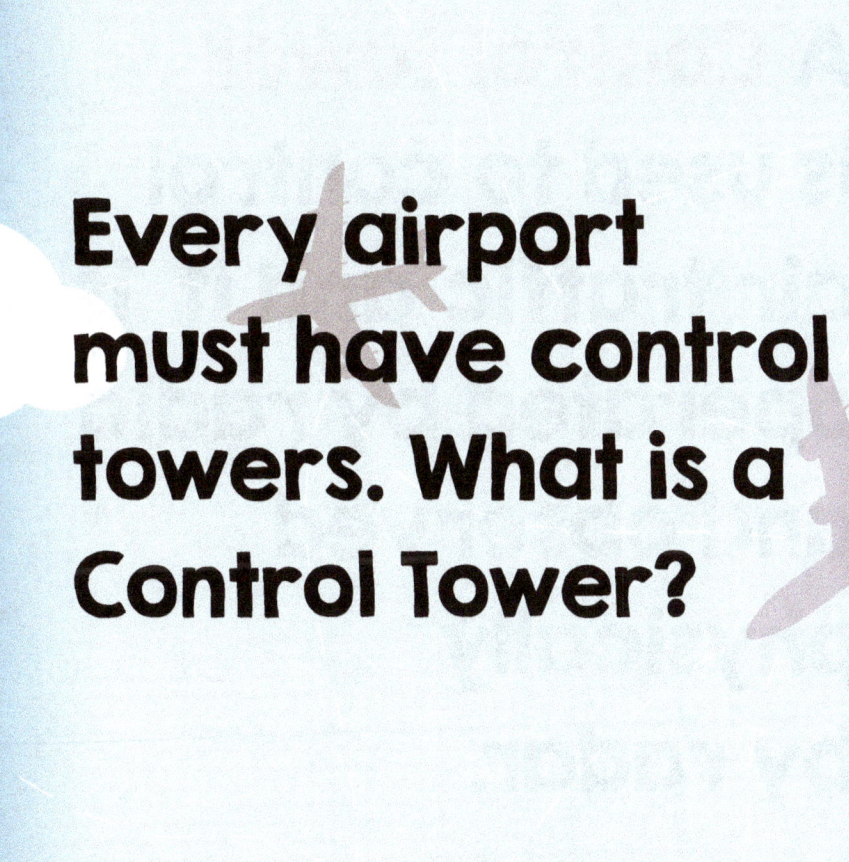

A **Control tower** is used to control air traffic and it is operated by radio and observed physically by radar.

This is what a control tower looks like.

A control tower is nothing without this group of people. Who are they?

They are the Air Traffic Controllers and they help the pilots maneuver their aircraft when taking off and landing.

They help the pilot out by using cool gadgets and devices like radars, computers, headphone radio and many more.

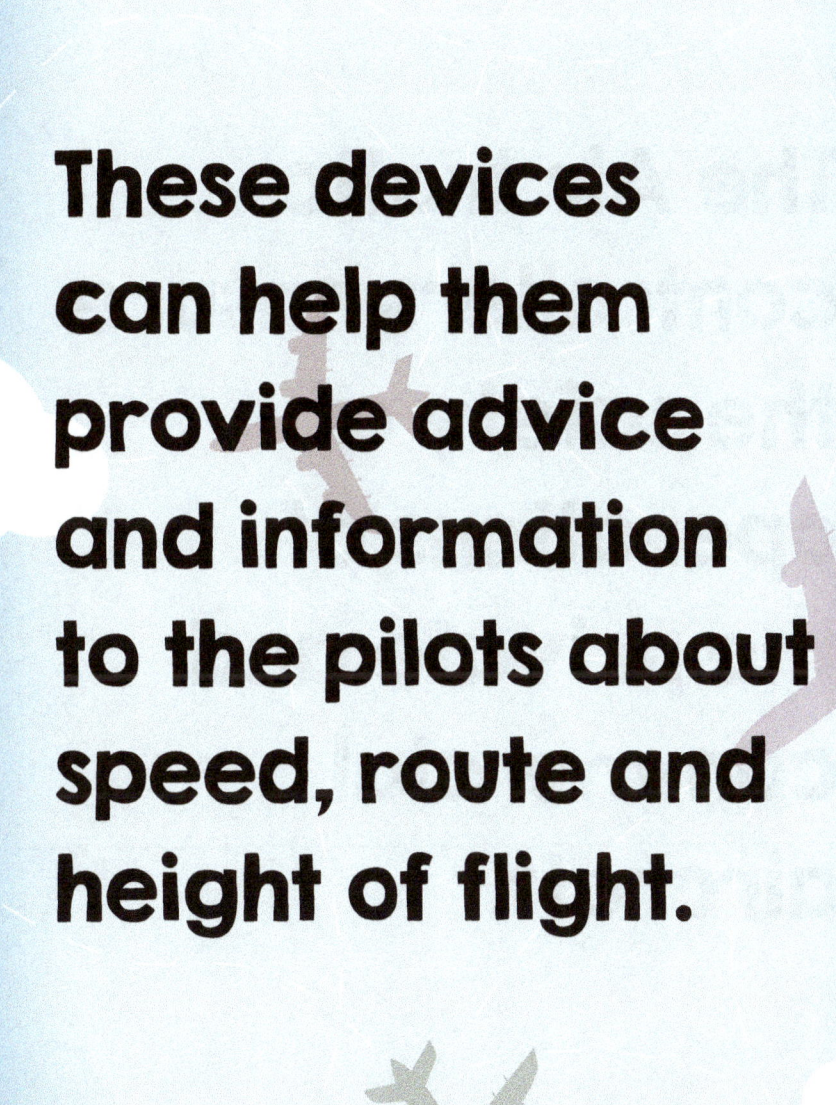

These devices can help them provide advice and information to the pilots about speed, route and height of flight.

The Air trafic controllers ensure the safety of operations of the private and commercial aircraft.

They direct the flights whenever there is bad weather.

They ensure that the traffic will flow smoothly with minimal delays.

Generally, the Air traffic controller's job is classified into 3 Sections:

- **Separation**
- **Direction**
- **Information**

SEPARATION

The controllers tell the pilots when they are too close to other planes. Their promptness ensures safe air transport, thereby saving the lives of the passengers.

DIRECTION

The traffic controllers will inform the pilots when it is their turn to take off.

INFORMATION

The air traffic controllers can give any advice to help ensure a safe trip.

The **pilot** can contact the air traffic controllers whenever he needs information on the weather and the conditions on the ground.

You will find these amazing people in these towers!

www.ingramcontent.com/pod-product-compliance
Lightning Source LLC
LaVergne TN
LVHW061321060426
835507LV00019B/2256